100
GREAT PASTA
SAUCES

100 GREAT PASTA SAUCES

SALLY GRIFFITHS

PHOTOGRAPHS BY
SIMON WHEELER

CASSELLPAPERBACKS

CONTENTS

INTRODUCTION

In the early Sixties my mother bought a small Italian 'casetta di campagna' in Calabria. With the house came Anna, much to my mother's surprise and delight, for Anna quickly established herself as confidante, counsellor, cook, the lot. For me, she soon showed that above all else she was an expert with pasta, and I've enjoyed her recipes ever since.

At that time southern Italy was the unjustly neglected reservoir of honest cooking, although the ingredients in this sunny, sea-encompassed area were extensive. Fruits and vegetables thrived in the strong sunshine, and fish and shellfish were plentiful; on the other hand, good beef was scarce. With limited meat resources Anna, in common with other Italian housewives, learnt how to stretch and vary the flavour of the pasta sauces and fillings by using generous quantities of fresh local ingredients. As Anna says, 'a meal need not be elaborate, it only has to be good.'

In my experience pasta dishes are the answer to last-minute suppers and just the thing to set the scene for an elaborate gourmet display. After a long day few of us have either the requisite mood or energy to cope with complicated recipes. With these human frailties in mind I have based my recipes on Anna's expertise. You will find them quick to prepare, easy to cook, delicious to look at and wonderful to eat.

Depending on whether a sauce is oil-based, cheese-based, vegetable-based or meat-based, it should be combined with a certain shape of pasta to obtain the correct balance of texture and flavours. I have therefore outlined a few useful combinations.

Cooking pasta is easy but it has to be just right. In simple question-and-answer form I have explained the basic technique so you can get it spot on every time!

Now that supermarkets stock a good range of Italian products we can widen our horizons. To this end I have compiled a list of ingredients for the storecupboard to enable you to make at least 30 of the recipes without dashing to the shops. I have also included a short, comprehensive list of utensils, highlighting one or two I find invaluable.

The rest of the book is dedicated to the recipes themselves, and although they are neither long nor complicated I have donated a few pages to really simple recipes that require little or no cooking. Thereafter the book is divided into chapters on sauces made with vegetables, eggs and cheese, fish, meat, and game.

With each recipe I have suggested an appropriate shape of pasta to complement the sauce, but as there are over 350 different varieties to choose from, the best way to find out which one you prefer is to experiment.

I have yet to come across anyone who has written about pasta who is not passionate about the subject themselves, and I feel no differently. It has given me enormous pleasure to write this book and I sincerely hope you will enjoy sampling the sauces as much as I did!

UTENSILS

Many of the utensils listed below form part of the everyday kitchen. However, if you don't already have them, it is worth investing in a large colander and, more importantly, a large heavy-based stainless steel saucepan for cooking pasta.

Large heavy-based stainless steel saucepan A large saucepan allows the water to circulate freely, preventing the pasta reabsorbing starch lost during cooking.

Large colander with base and handles Large amounts of pasta drained in a small colander will just slip over the sides, whereas a large colander will enable you to drain, shake and return the pasta to the warm pot efficiently and quickly.

Garlic crusher Invest in a sturdy crusher, which empties the pulp easily because you'll be using it a great deal!

Cheese grater You don't need anything elaborate: a simple metal grater is fine.

Lemon squeezer Buy one with a guard to prevent the pips falling into the sauce.

Measuring jug Invest in a jug which indicates metric and imperial measurements clearly.

Metal tablespoon and teaspoon Many quantities are measured in these standard spoons.

Heavy-based frying pans Sturdy pans will ensure an even temperature, and they will last for years.

Food processor This is a real time-saver.

Long-handled wooden spoons With these you can stir the pasta in the large pot easily.

Long-handled forks These are invaluable when you are testing long, slippery strands of pasta.

Parmesan knife The short, sharp blade can pare slices from large pieces of Parmesan.

Potato peeler Use it to make curls of Parmesan cheese for salads or decoration.

Pepper grinder Choose one to complement your table setting. Grinders come in wood, silver or plastic and many attractive colours.

Small wooden spoons These are less abrasive than metal ones.

Small saucepan A few small saucepans are invaluable.

Chopping boards They prevent worksurfaces from becoming damaged or scratched.

Storage jars These are useful for keeping dry pasta once the packet has been opened.

Plastic chopping board Use this to chop garlic or any other ingredient with a strong smell.

Long-handled rubber spatula Use it to scrape mixtures down the sides of the blender or food processor.

Knives Really sharp knives make chopping and slicing much easier.

Bowls A good selection of bowls is useful for mixing ingredients.

Pestle and mortar Crushing peppercorns or small amounts of herbs in a mortar is a simple yet effective way of releasing the full flavour of the ingredient.

Slotted spoon This is useful for lifting and draining cooked stuffed pasta shapes.

THE STORECUPBOARD

Although fresh produce is generally considered superior, many canned goods are perfectly acceptable for pasta sauces. Most of the ingredients listed below are available in supermarkets. Alternatively, head for a good Italian delicatessen and indulge!

Dried pasta

Keep a variety of different shapes and sizes such as: capelli d'angelo, spaghetti, linguine or trenette, bucatini, fettuccine, tagliatelle, fusilli, farfalle, conchiglie, penne, rigatoni and tortellini.

General ingredients

Anchovies, sardines, canned salmon, canned tuna, canned vongole, mustard, jars of roasted peppers (pimientos), green olives, pitted black olives, capers, canned beans such as flageolet, dried porcini, sun-dried tomatoes (packed dry or in olive oil), canned tomatoes (at least 4 cans), tomato purée, natural dried breadcrumbs, red and white wine.

Nuts and seeds

Store in tightly sealed containers or they will go soft.
Pine nuts, flaked almonds, walnuts, poppyseeds.

Oils and vinegars

Keep well sealed, away from the light.
Extra virgin olive oil, truffle oil, walnut or hazelnut oil, chilli oil, light olive oil (for frying), balsamic vinegar, white wine vinegar.

Pastes

To keep paste in jars fresh, pour a thin layer of olive oil over the surface.
Green olive paste, black olive paste, tomato paste.

Pepper and salt

Store in a cool, dry place. To prevent salt absorbing water, mix with a few grains of rice.
Black peppercorns, sea salt (fine and coarsely ground).

Spices

Store in airtight containers in a cool, dry, dark place.
Chilli flakes, nutmeg, cinnamon, saffron threads.

Dried herbs

Store in airtight containers in a cool, dry, dark place.
Marjoram, oregano, tarragon, thyme, rosemary, basil, bay leaves, dill.

Fresh herbs

Grow them in a window box or in pretty pots on the window sill.
Basil, coriander, flat leaf parsley, chives.

Fruit and vegetable bowl

Tomatoes, lemons, garlic, onions, shallots, peppers, chillies.

Bacon and ham

Prosciutto (buy in vacuum-sealed pack and store in the fridge), pancetta (keep tightly wrapped in the fridge).

In the fridge

Parmesan and pecorino romano cheese (keep tightly wrapped), crème fraîche (keeps longer than ordinary cream), butter, cream, eggs.

In the freezer

Packet of peas; fresh veal, vegetable, chicken and fish stocks (available from supermarkets).

Bucatini

Tagliatelle

Fusilli lunghi bucati

Spaghetti

Maccheroni napoletani

Trenette

PASTA SHAPES

Pasta comes in hundreds of different shapes, and in Italy the combination of flavour,

texture and shape is taken very seriously. For example:

ong round pasta –

ıch as capelli d'angelo, fedelini, spaghettini, vermicelli, spaghetti or
ıaghettoni, needs an olive-oil-based sauce to keep the strands slippery
ıd separate.

ong flat pasta –

nguine, trenette, fettuccine, tagliatelle, bucatini, tagliolini, lasagnette,
ıodles, lasagne and tonnarelli, for example – should be accompanied
y a heavier sauce based on cheese, eggs and/or cream or one that
ıntains small pieces of meat such as prosciutto.

Short pasta –

i.e. shaped and tubular pasta – is best served with a juicy sauce that
will penetrate into the pasta hollows. Shaped and medium-sized
tubular pasta are excellent with vegetable-based sauces, and larger
examples, such as penne rigate or macaroni, are ideal in baked dishes
or with rich meat sauces.

Filled pasta –

these envelopes of pasta may be stuffed with a variety of delicious
ingredients. It is best to keep the sauce simple so that it does not
overpower the flavour of the filling – a little melted butter and cheese,
for example.

Tortellini

Liasagne

Tagliarini

Fettuccine

Ravioli

Ravioli alla ricot

ALL ABOUT PASTA

Beware the pronouncements of any self-styled historian-cum-gastronome who speaks authoritatively of the origins of pasta cuisine, probably citing some esoteric corner of Italy. The simple fact is that nobody knows where or how pasta came our way. What is certain, however, is that pasta came to the West. One misty legend has it that pasta originated in Chinese kitchens and that Marco Polo returned from his oriental travels with know-how concerning pasta dishes and the talent for passing on his priceless expertise to others.

hatever, whenever and wherever the origins of pasta, its appetizing vours have enlivened first Italian and then the Western world's les ever since. Little wonder that most of us think of pasta as equivocally Italian – they took to pasta as if to pasta born.

ow many different shapes of pasta are there? The Italians have vented over 350 different shapes of pasta, each one suitable for a rtain sauce (see page 13).

ould pasta be served as a starter or a main course? It can be hot, ld, a starter, main course, even a pudding. Italians sometimes serve a hall helping of pasta between the fish and meat course.

pasta good for you? Pasta contains protein, vitamins and minerals. is high in carbohydrates and helps athletes sustain their energy level.

pasta fattening? Pasta on its own is not. It's the accompanying sauce hich sends the calories spiralling upwards!

there an alternative to wheat-based pasta? Try spelt-based pasta ou will find it in healthfood shops). It is low in gluten and can be ten by anybody with an allergy to wheat.

hich is best, fresh or dried pasta? Dried pasta is considered by many be just as good as fresh. However, it is important to use a good ality Italian brand.

ow can you tell freshly made pasta? Just make sure it comes from a ll-recommended source because extra water is often added to crease the weight. Also, there is no way of telling how long pasta has en on the shelf – an inferior quality will swell considerably during oking and end up a sticky mass.

hat type of sauce is served with fresh pasta? A light sauce corporating cream, butter or any ingredient which will be absorbed the porous surface of the dough.

What is the advantage of dried pasta? It keeps for at least a year and comes in an enormous variety of different shapes and sizes.

Is fresh pasta considered more authentic than dried? Not really. Today fresh pasta is only sold in the north of Italy, whereas in the south they eat vast quantities of dried pasta.

How do you know which pasta to use with which sauce? As a general rule, long round pasta is served with oil-based sauces, flat pasta with sauces based on eggs, cheese, cream or light meats, and shaped and tubular pasta with thicker sauces which can penetrate the hollows.

How long does pasta keep? Dried pasta will keep for approximately one year whereas fresh pasta is best eaten on the day of purchase.

How is dried pasta made? The basic dough is made with durum wheat ground into semolina and mixed to a paste with water (some pastas include eggs). Make sure you buy a good Italian brand because inferior makes of pasta sometimes split during cooking – look out for the words *durum wheat* or *pura semolina* on the packet.

What is the difference between 'fresh pasta' found in supermarkets, and home-made pasta? 'Fresh pasta' (made with durum wheat, semolina, flour, eggs and water) in supermarkets does not really compare with home-made pasta, which has a lightness and delicacy of its own.

What is durum wheat flour? Durum wheat is grown mostly in Canada and the United States. When ground down it forms a hard semolina which gives the pasta its firm texture.

What is the difference between pasta made with eggs and without eggs? Pasta made with eggs is slightly richer in taste and colour. Eggs add protein and give the pasta extra texture.

15

COOKING PASTA

At what stage do you cook the pasta? Cook it *just* before serving.

How much pasta per person? Much depends on your appetite! The following amounts are for four people.

As a starter :

Dried pasta: 175–225 g (6–8 oz)

Fresh pasta: 450–700 g (1–1¹/₂ lb)

As a main course:

Dried pasta: 350 g (12 oz)

Fresh pasta: 900 g (2 lb)

How do you cook pasta? Bring a large saucepan of water to the boil, add salt and then the pasta and stir well. Put the lid on the saucepan until the water returns to boiling point, then remove it. Stir the pasta several times during the cooking process. To make sure the pasta does not overcook, test it – once or twice – a minute or two before the manufacturer's recommended cooking time is up. Then drain, return the pasta to the saucepan and stir in a little olive oil. Toss with the sauce and serve immediately.

For cold pasta cook as above, then drain and toss with a little olive oil. Allow to cool at room temperature.

Which kind of saucepan is best for cooking pasta? To make sure pasta cooks evenly and does not stick together, use a heavy-based saucepan which is large enough to allow the water to circulate around the pasta and remain at a constant temperature.

How much water do you need? During the cooking process pasta absorbs water and loses starch. If there is insufficient water in the saucepan the pasta will reabsorb the starch. Work on a ratio of 1 litre (1³/₄ pints) of water to 100 g (3¹/₂ oz) pasta.

Should the water be salted? Yes, otherwise the pasta will taste rather bland. Add 1 teaspoon of salt per litre (1³/₄ pints) of water.

How do you prevent pasta sticking to the pot? Some people add a little olive oil to the water before putting in the pasta, but this is not normally necessary. (Only large flat pieces of pasta need a dash of oil in the water.) As soon as you put the pasta into boiling water stir well, then stir again several times during the cooking process.

How long does pasta take to cook? Fresh pasta cooks in approximately 2–3 minutes (stuffed pasta takes a little longer), whereas dried pasta can take anything from 4 to 15 minutes, depending on its size and shape.

How can you tell when pasta is cooked? Using a fork, take out a piece of pasta once or twice before the recommended cooking time is up and test. Pasta should be cooked but *al dente* which means *firm to the bite*.

Can you overcook pasta? Pasta becomes a soft sticky mass if cooked for too long. The only thing to do is throw it away and start again!

Should you use a sieve or a colander to drain pasta ? As soon the pasta is cooked, tip it into a large colander, give a few shakes and return the pasta to the saucepan or put it in a preheated dish. Do not over-drain pasta should be slippery so that the sauce coats it properly. To drain stuffed pasta, lift it out of the water with a slotted spoon.

Do you pour cold water over pasta after draining it? No. It would remove the coating of starch. Sprinkle with olive oil or a few knobs of butter to keep the strands slippery, then toss pasta and sauce together.

When do you add the sauce to the pasta? As soon as the pasta is drained, toss it with the sauce. For stuffed pasta, which might break if tossed, either pour the sauce into a dish and lay the pasta on top or gently spoon the sauce over the pasta.

How much sauce should be served with pasta? Not too much. The sauce is only intended to coat the pasta; it should not swim around in it.

Are there any traditional accompaniments to serve with pasta? Grated Parmesan is sprinkled over most pasta dishes (except those with fish-based sauces). Do this just before eating because Parmesan loses its flavour and aroma within minutes. Other garnishes include freshly ground black pepper, pecorino cheese, toasted pine nuts (see below) and freshly chopped herbs.

HOW TO:

Roast nuts and seeds Toss them around in a hot, dry frying pan until they are lightly browned.

Skin tomatoes Put the tomatoes in a large bowl of boiling water and leave for 1–2 minutes. Remove, and the skin will peel off easily.

Skin peppers Roast peppers in a preheated 200°C, 400°F, Gas Mark 6 oven for 25–30 minutes (or place under a hot grill), until the skins become blistered and black. Remove, put them in a polythene bag, seal, cool and then skin.

Sweat To 'sweat' means sauté for a few minutes until the ingredients become transparent.

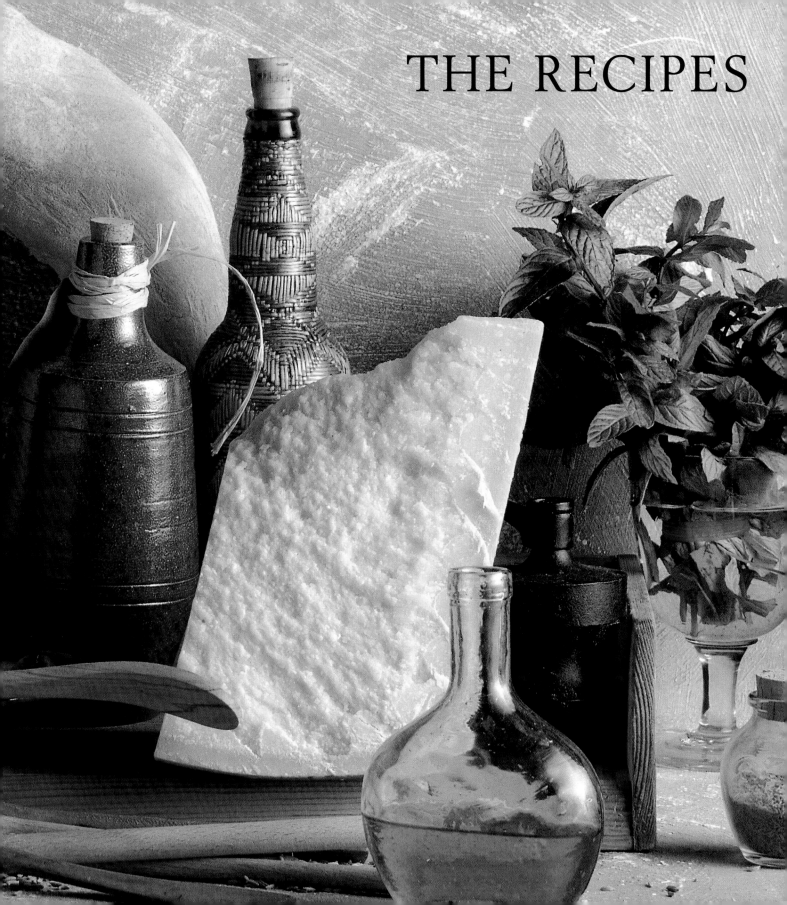

THE RECIPES

PESTO

All recipes are for four people. Bursting with flavour, these aromatic sauces have a wonderful, voluptuous consistency. Serve with spaghetti or a long flat pasta such as trenette, tagliatelle or fettuccine. (Delicious with hot or cold pasta.)

• Pesto can be kept for 1 week in an airtight container in the refrigerator.

• Too much blending will ruin the lovely nutty texture.

ROCKET PESTO

50 g (2 oz) pine nuts	9 tablespoons extra virgin olive oil
50 g (2 oz) fresh rocket, stalks included	TO FINISH
1/2–2 cloves garlic, peeled and crushed	Freshly ground black pepper
50 g (2 oz) Parmesan, freshly grated	25 g (1 oz) pine nuts, toasted (see page 17)
1 tablespoon lemon juice	Freshly grated Parmesan
Salt	

Place all the ingredients, except the oil, in a food processor and blend for 30 seconds or until roughly chopped. Then slowly pour in the oil, and blend until smooth.

Toss with pasta, season with pepper and sprinkle with toasted pine nuts and Parmesan.

• Try walnut pieces instead of pine nuts.

• Use raw baby spinach instead of rocket.

• If the sauce is too dry, add more oil.

BASIL PESTO

50 g (2 oz) fresh basil leaves	TO FINISH
1 clove garlic, peeled and crushed	Salt and freshly ground black pepper
1 tablespoon pine nuts	25 g (1 oz) Parmesan, freshly grated
6 tablespoons extra virgin olive oil	

Put all the ingredients, except the oil, in a food processor and blend for 30 seconds, or until roughly chopped. Then slowly pour in the oil and blend until smooth.

Toss with pasta, season and sprinkle with Parmesan.

• If the sauce is too dry add more oil and blend for a few seconds.

PARSLEY AND HAZELNUT PESTO

50 g (2 oz) fresh parsley (weight without stalks)	6 tablespoons hazelnut oil
25 g (1 oz) Parmesan, freshly grated	6 tablespoons groundnut oil
2 cloves garlic, peeled and crushed	TO FINISH
1 tablespoon lemon juice	2 tablespoons hazelnuts, chopped
Salt and freshly ground black pepper	Freshly grated Parmesan

Make as for Basil Pesto.

OLIVE AND PISTACHIO PESTO

50 g (2 oz) unsalted pistachio nuts	1 tablespoon lemon juice
4 cloves garlic, peeled and crushed	100 g (4 oz) Parmesan, freshly grated
1 tablespoon green peppercorns, drained	Salt and freshly ground black pepper
100 g (4 oz) pitted black or green olives	8 tablespoons olive oil

Make as for Basil Pesto.

SORREL PESTO

100 g (4 oz) sorrel	TO FINISH
50 g (2 oz) pine nuts, toasted (see page 17)	Salt and freshly ground black pepper
50 g (2 oz) Parmesan, freshly grated	Freshly grated Parmesan
2 tablespoons extra virgin olive oil	

Make as for Basil Pesto.

SUN-DRIED TOMATO PESTO

1 1/2 tablespoons sun-dried tomatoes, reconstituted in warm water or drained of oil, chopped	2 cloves garlic, peeled and crushed
	1 tablespoon lemon juice
	Salt
2 tablespoons fresh parsley (without stalks)	4 tablespoons extra virgin olive oil
1 1/2 tablespoons pitted black olives	TO FINISH
65 g (2 1/2 oz) pine nuts	Salt and freshly ground black pepper
2 shallots, chopped	Freshly grated Parmesan

Make as for Basil Pesto.

MIXED HERB PESTO

100 g (4 oz) fresh parsley (weight without stalks)	1 tablespoon onion, chopped
	25 g (1 oz) fresh breadcrumbs
15 g (1/2 oz) fresh basil leaves	3 tablespoons lemon juice
50 g (2 oz) canned anchovies, drained and rinsed	7 tablespoons extra virgin olive oil
	TO FINISH
3 tablespoons capers	Salt and freshly ground black pepper
2 cloves garlic, peeled and crushed	Freshly grated Parmesan

Make as for Basil Pesto.

CORIANDER PESTO

50 g (2 oz) fresh coriander leaves	8 tablespoons extra virgin olive oil
1 tablespoon pine nuts	TO FINISH
1/2–1 teaspoon dried chilli flakes	Salt and freshly ground black pepper
1 tablespoon lemon juice	Freshly grated Parmesan

Make as for Basil Pesto.

Right: Rocket Pes

OIL AND BUTTER BASED SAUCES

All recipes are for four people.

Oil- and butter-based sauces served with long round pasta, a delicious salad and plenty of fresh bread are the perfect answer to an impromptu meal. Straight from the storecupboard, they are quick and easy to make and the flavours of the ingredients are beautifully accentuated. Oil- and butter-based sauces are particularly suited to stuffed pastas.

OIL AND GARLIC

ablespoons extra virgin olive oil
loves garlic, peeled and finely chopped

Salt and freshly ground black pepper
Freshly grated Parmesan

a small pan over a low heat *barely warm* the olive oil, then add the lic and *warm gently* for a further 30 seconds. Toss the garlic oil with t pasta, season and sprinkle with Parmesan.

OIL, GARLIC AND HERB

ablespoons extra virgin olive oil
loves garlic, peeled and finely chopped
blespoon fresh parsley, finely chopped

1 tablespoon fresh basil leaves, torn into strips
Salt and freshly ground black pepper
Freshly grated Parmesan

a small pan over a low heat *barely warm* the olive oil, then add garlic and *warm gently* for a further 30 seconds. Toss the garlic oil d herbs with hot pasta, mixing together well. Season and sprinkle th Parmesan.

As an alternative, replace the parsley and basil with 2 tablespoons opped fresh chives or oregano.

Add a handful of toasted pine nuts (see page 17) with the herbs for a unchier texture.

OIL AND CORIANDER

ablespoons extra virgin olive oil
love garlic, peeled and finely chopped
ablespoons fresh coriander, chopped

Salt and freshly ground black pepper
Freshly grated Parmesan

a small pan over a low heat *barely warm* the olive oil, then add garlic d *warm gently* for a further 30 seconds. Toss the garlic oil and riander with hot pasta, season and sprinkle with Parmesan.

TRUFFLE OIL

ablespoons truffle oil
t and freshly ground black pepper

Freshly grated Parmesan

a small heavy-based pan *gently warm* the oil, then toss with hot sta, season and sprinkle with Parmesan.

Excellent with stuffed pasta such as ravioli.

OIL, CHILLI AND GARLIC

8 tablespoons extra virgin olive oil
1 clove garlic, peeled and crushed

2 teaspoons dried chilli flakes

Heat the oil in a small, heavy-based pan over a moderate heat, add the garlic and cook for 30 seconds or until golden. Remove the garlic with a slotted spoon and discard. Add the chilli flakes to the garlic-flavoured oil and toss with hot pasta. Season, and add a little more oil if desired.

BUTTER AND PARMESAN

100 g (4 oz) butter
3 tablespoons freshly grated Parmesan

Freshly ground black pepper

Gently melt the butter in a small saucepan over a low heat, then toss with hot pasta. Stir in the Parmesan and season with pepper.

CHIVE BUTTER

100 g (4 oz) butter
15 g (1/2 oz) fresh chives, chopped

Salt and freshly ground black pepper
Freshly grated Parmesan

Melt the butter in a small saucepan over a low heat. Add the chives, stir and toss with hot pasta. Season and sprinkle with Parmesan.

BROWNED BUTTER AND GARLIC

100 g (4 oz) butter
3–4 cloves garlic, peeled and crushed

Freshly ground black pepper
100 g (4 oz) Parmesan, freshly grated

In a heavy-based pan heat the butter until it starts to foam. Add the garlic and, stirring constantly, fry for 1-2 minutes or until golden brown. Toss with hot pasta, season with pepper and stir in the Parmesan.

BUTTER AND TOASTED POPPYSEED

100 g (4 oz) butter
2 1/2 tablespoons poppyseeds, toasted (see page 17)

Salt and freshly ground black pepper
Freshly grated Parmesan

Gently melt the butter in a small saucepan over a low heat, then toss with hot pasta. Add the poppyseeds and mix together well. Season and sprinkle with Parmesan.

CREAM, EGG AND CHEESE SAUCES

All recipes are for four people.

CREAM AND BLACK OLIVE SAUCE

The dramatic combination of black and white makes this a wonderful sauce for a dinner party. Try it with fettuccine, and a crisp green salad.

3 tablespoons pitted black olives	1 clove garlic, peeled
2 sprigs fresh thyme, leaves only	1 tablespoon olive oil
1 teaspoon mixed dried herbs	40 g (1 1/2 oz) butter
4 baby gherkins	600 ml (1 pint) single cream or crème fraîche

Put the olives, thyme, mixed herbs, gherkins, garlic and olive oil in a food processor and blend to a paste. Melt the butter in a small saucepan over a low heat, then add the paste and blend together well. Stir in the cream and cook for about 5 minutes or until the sauce has reduced a little.

Toss with hot pasta and serve.

CARBONARA SAUCE

Eggs with bacon is a tried and tested favourite. Serve this sauce with bucatini or spaghetti, and a tomato salad.

50 g (2 oz) butter or 4 tablespoons olive oil	1 tablespoon milk
100 g (4 oz) pancetta or smoked streaky bacon,	40 g (1 1/2 oz) pecorino cheese, freshly grated
rind removed, cut into small strips	Salt and freshly ground black pepper
4 egg yolks	Freshly grated Parmesan

Heat the butter or oil in a heavy-based pan over a low heat and fry the pancetta or bacon for 10 minutes or until lightly brown (be careful not to burn it). Remove the pancetta or bacon with a slotted spoon and place in a deep, warm bowl. Put the egg yolks, milk and cheese in a small bowl and lightly beat with a fork to mix. Pour the mixture over the bacon, add the hot pasta and toss together well. Season, and sprinkle with grated Parmesan.

EGG AND HERB SAUCE

One of the most simple yet sophisticated sauces in the book. Serve with pasta shells or fusilli.

2 tablespoons fresh parsley, chopped	1 teaspoon capers, chopped
2 tablespoons fresh basil, chopped	6 hard-boiled egg yolks, cooled and sieved
2 tablespoons fresh chervil, chopped	6 tablespoons extra virgin olive oil
2 tablespoons fresh chives, chopped	Salt and freshly ground black pepper

Mix together all the ingredients in a bowl, season and toss with hot pasta.

• This can also be served cold.

CREAM, PORCINI AND SHERRY SAUCE

This ambrosial sauce is irresistible! Serve with a long flat pasta such as pappardelle, and a rocket salad.

20 g (3/4 oz) dried porcini	2 shallots, finely chopped
90 ml (3 fl oz) sherry	350 ml (12 fl oz) double cream
90 ml (3 fl oz) madeira	Salt and freshly ground black pepper
40 g (1 1/2 oz) butter	1 1/2 tablespoons fresh chives, chopped
2 cloves garlic, peeled and finely chopped	

Soak the porcini in the sherry and madeira for 15 minutes, then drain, taking care to leave any grit at the bottom of the bowl, and reserve the liquid.

Melt the butter in a heavy-based pan over a moderate heat and gently fry the garlic and shallots for 3 minutes. Add the porcini and cook for minute. Turn up the heat and stir in the cream and reserved liquid. Cook for 5 minutes or until the sauce is creamy and thick.

Season, toss with hot pasta and sprinkle with chives.

BLUE CHEESE AND BROCCOLI SAUCE WITH TOASTED NUTS

The shapes, colours and textures in this wonderful sauce complement each other beautifully. Serve with a large pasta shape such as penne rigate, and plenty of bread to mop up the sauce!

225 g (8 oz) small broccoli florets	Salt and freshly ground black pepper
1 tablespoon olive oil	100 g (4 oz) cambozola or blue brie,
1 small onion, finely chopped	chopped into small pieces
150 ml (5 fl oz) dry white wine	2 tablespoons flaked almonds, toasted
4 tablespoons double cream	(see page 17)

Cook the broccoli in salted boiling water for 3–4 minutes. Drain and put aside in a warm bowl.

Heat the oil in a heavy-based pan and gently fry the onion for 3 minutes. Add the wine and cream, bring to the boil and reduce a little then season and stir in the cheese.

Toss the broccoli with hot pasta, then gently mix in the sauce. Sprinkle with the almonds and serve.

Right: Carbonara Sau

STILTON, RED WINE AND WALNUT SAUCE

Serve this rich, velvety sauce with pappardelle, and a salad of radicchio, chicory and celery.

350 ml (12 fl oz) double cream
90 ml (3 fl oz) red wine or port
350 g (12 oz) stilton cheese, crumbled
Salt and freshly ground black pepper

150 g (5 oz) walnut pieces, toasted
(see page 17) and chopped
4–6 tablespoon fresh parsley, chopped

Put the cream in a large saucepan and bring to the boil. Add the wine or port, reduce the heat and simmer for 5 minutes. Add the stilton and simmer for 3 minutes or until the cheese has melted and the sauce thickens. Season, toss with hot pasta, and sprinkle with walnuts and parsley.

MOZZARELLA, TOMATO AND CHILLI SAUCE

The combination of red and white makes this an eye-catching sauce. Serve with fusilli, and some hot ciabatta bread.

4 tablespoons olive oil
2 cloves garlic, peeled and finely chopped
1 fresh red chilli, seeded and chopped
450 g (1 lb) ripe tomatoes, skinned
(see page 17), seeded and chopped

Salt and freshly ground black pepper
100 g (4 oz) mozzarella cheese,
cut into 1 cm (1/2 inch) cubes

Put the oil in a heavy-based pan and over a moderate heat gently fry the garlic and chilli for 1 minute (be careful not to burn the garlic). Turn up the heat, add the tomatoes and season. Cook for 4 minutes, stirring occasionally. Toss the sauce and mozzarella with hot pasta and serve at once.

DOLCELATTE AND WALNUT SAUCE

This creamy sauce has a lovely nutty texture. Serve with a chicory salad and plenty of ciabatta bread to mop up the sauce.

100 ml (3 1/2 fl oz) double cream
175 g (6 oz) dolcelatte cheese
50 g (2 oz) walnut pieces

Salt and freshly ground black pepper
1 tablespoon fresh basil leaves, torn into strips

Gently heat the cream and cheese in a heavy-based pan over a moderate heat, stirring constantly. When melted and smooth, add the nuts and mix together well. Season. Remove from the heat, stir in the basil and toss with hot pasta.

Try pecan nuts instead of walnuts.

RICOTTA AND TOMATO SAUCE

This delicate sauce is excellent for a light supper dish. Serve with linguine, and a salad of rocket and freshly shaved pecorino cheese.

5 tablespoons extra virgin olive oil
4 spring onions, chopped,
or 5 tablespoons fresh chives, chopped
225 g (8 oz) ricotta cheese,
crumbled or cut into cubes
3 tablespoons freshly grated Parmesan,
plus more for serving

4 ripe tomatoes, skinned (see page 17),
seeded and diced
6 tablespoons fresh basil leaves,
torn into strips
Salt and freshly ground black pepper

Heat the oil in a heavy-based pan over a very low heat. Add the spring onions or chives, ricotta and Parmesan and mix together well. Cook for 1 minute, then stir in tomatoes, basil and seasoning. As soon as the sauce start to warm, remove from the heat, toss with hot pasta and sprinkle with Parmesan.

RICOTTA AND BUTTER SAUCE

A light, fluffy sauce, this is excellent with tagliatelle, and a crisp green salad.

100 g (4 oz) butter
550 g (1 1/4 lb) ricotta cheese, crumbled

Salt
Mixed (coloured) peppercorns, freshly ground

Melt the butter in a small saucepan over a moderate heat, and pour over hot pasta. Sprinkle the ricotta over the top, season with salt and toss well. Serve with freshly ground multi-coloured peppercorns.

MASCARPONE AND WALNUT SAUCE

Creamy and crunchy, this sauce has a good combination of textures and flavours. Serve with large penne, and a bacon and spinach salad.

50 g (2 oz) butter
1 clove garlic, peeled and crushed
200 g (7 oz) walnut pieces

250 g (9 oz) mascarpone cheese
60 g (2 1/2 oz) Parmesan, freshly grated
Salt and freshly ground black pepper

Melt the butter in a heavy-based pan and over a moderate heat fry the garlic for 30 seconds or until golden. Add the walnuts and gently toss around for 3–4 minutes. Then stir in the mascarpone and keep stirring until it has completely melted. Fold in the Parmesan, season and toss with hot pasta.

EGG AND CAPER SAUCE

Straight out of the storecupboard! Try this egg-based sauce with spaghettini or tagliolini.

25 g (1 oz) butter, softened
3 eggs, size 1, lightly beaten
100 g (4 oz) pecorino cheese, freshly grated

1 tablespoon capers, drained and rinsed
1 tablespoon fresh parsley, chopped
Salt and freshly ground black pepper

Put all the ingredients in a bowl and mix together well. Season and toss with hot pasta.

Left: Blue Cheese and Broccoli Sauce with Toasted Nuts

CREAM AND LEMON SAUCE

The tangy flavour of lemon adds a perfect contrast in this delicate, creamy sauce. Serve with festoni, and a radicchio salad.

25 g (1 oz) butter
250 ml (8 fl oz) double cream
2 tablespoons lemon zest, grated

2 tablespoons Parmesan cheese, freshly grated
1 tablespoon pine nuts, toasted (see page 17)
Salt and freshly ground black pepper

Place the butter, cream and lemon zest in a small saucepan and bring to the boil. Once the liquid has reached boiling point, lower the heat, stir in the Parmesan and sprinkle with the pine nuts. Season and toss with hot pasta.

RICOTTA AND FRESH HERB SAUCE

Lots of fresh herbs mixed with ricotta make this sauce the perfect choice for a light supper dish. Serve with conchiglie, and a spinach salad.

450 g (1 lb) ricotta cheese
2 tablespoons Parmesan cheese, freshly grated
2 tablespoons fresh flat leaf parsley, chopped
2 tablespoons fresh basil, chopped

2 tablespoons fresh chives, chopped
2 tablespoons fresh oregano, chopped
Salt and freshly ground black pepper

Mix all the ingredients in a bowl, season and fold into hot pasta.

• This sauce can also be served with cold pasta.

CREME FRAICHE AND SUN-DRIED TOMATO SAUCE

Evoking memories of hot sunny days, this simple sauce can be served with penne or rigatoni, and a salad of frisé, chicory and fresh basil.

250 ml (8 fl oz) crème fraîche
Freshly ground black pepper

6 sun-dried tomatoes, reconstituted in warm water or drained of oil, then cut into thin strips
5 tablespoons sun-dried tomato purée

Combine the crème fraîche and tomato purée and mix together well. Stir in the sun-dried tomatoes, season and toss with hot pasta.

• This sauce can also be served with cold pasta or as a side dish on its own.

GOAT'S CHEESE AND TOMATO SAUCE

Shades of the Med! Serve this summery sauce with tagliatelle, and a salad of tomatoes, onion and juicy black olives.

700 g (1 1/2 lb) ripe tomatoes, skinned (see page 17), seeded and chopped
4 tablespoons fresh basil, coarsely chopped

150 g (5 oz) fresh goat's cheese, crumbled
6 tablespoons extra virgin olive oil
Salt and freshly ground black pepper

Combine all the ingredients in a large bowl, season and toss with hot pasta.

• Goat's cheese with herbs and garlic is a lovely alternative to plain goat's cheese.

• This sauce can also be served cold, as a dish on its own.

THREE CHEESE SAUCE

Throw this impressive sauce together in a flash. Serve with green tagliatelli or fettuccine, and a radicchio salad.

20 g (3/4 oz) butter
50 g (2 oz) dolcelatte or gorgonzola cheese, cut into small cubes
100 g (4 oz) mascarpone cheese

75 g (3 oz) Parmesan, freshly grated
1/4 teaspoon nutmeg, grated
10 large leaves fresh basil, torn into strips

Melt the butter in a heavy-based saucepan over a moderate heat. Add the cheeses and stir to mix together well. Toss with hot pasta and sprinkle with nutmeg and basil.

• Add a tablespoon of toasted flaked almonds or chopped walnuts for a crunchier texture.

Right: *Three Cheese Sauc*

VEGETABLE SAUCES

All recipes are for four people.

QUICK TOMATO SAUCE WITH CREAM AND SUN-DRIED TOMATOES

This simple sauce is bursting with flavour. Serve with penne, and a green bean salad.

1 tablespoon olive oil
1 clove garlic, peeled and crushed
400 g (14 oz) canned tomatoes, drained and chopped
1 teaspoon tomato purée
125 ml (4 fl oz) double cream

1 tablespoon sun-dried tomatoes, reconstituted in warm water or drained of oil, then finely chopped
1 teaspoon fresh flat leaf parsley, chopped
Salt and freshly ground black pepper

Heat the oil in a heavy-based pan and fry the garlic for 30 seconds or until pale golden. Add the tomatoes, turn up the heat and cook for 5 minutes. Then lower the heat and stir in the tomato purée. Add the cream and sun-dried tomatoes and simmer gently for a further 3 minutes.

Fold in the parsley, season and toss with hot pasta.

BLACK OLIVE AND CHILLI SAUCE

The provocative flavour of olives is accentuated by marinating them overnight. Serve with linguine, and a tomato salad.

• Remember to marinate the olives overnight.

5 tablespoons extra virgin olive oil
185 g (6 1/2 oz) pitted black olives, chopped
1/2 teaspoon dried chilli flakes

2 cloves garlic, peeled and finely chopped
1 tablespoon fresh parsley, chopped
Salt and freshly ground black pepper

Mix 2 tablespoons of the oil with the olives, chilli flakes and garlic in a bowl and leave to marinate overnight.

The next day, heat the remaining oil in a heavy-based pan and add the marinated olive mixture, parsley and a little salt. Simmer gently for 5 minutes. Season and toss with hot pasta.

• This sauce can also be served with cold pasta.

OYSTER MUSHROOM SAUCE

High in flavour, low in calories! Serve with capelli d'angeli, and a watercress and orange salad.

4 tablespoons sesame oil
1 leek, cut lengthways into very fine strips
12 spring onions, green ends only, chopped
1 clove garlic, peeled and crushed
2 tablespoons soy sauce
125 ml (4 fl oz) fresh orange juice
1 cm (1/2 inch) strip lemon zest

1/2 teaspoon sugar
1 teaspoon sherry vinegar
1/4 teaspoon five spice powder
125 g (4 1/2 oz) oyster mushrooms
TO FINISH
Salt and freshly ground black pepper
2 tablespoons sesame seeds, toasted (see page 17)

Heat 2 tablespoons of the sesame oil in a frying pan, add the leeks and, turning constantly, fry until the strips become dark brown and crispy. Remove with a slotted spoon, drain on kitchen paper and set aside.

Heat the remaining sesame oil in a large frying pan and gently fry the spring onions and garlic for 1–2 minutes. Add the soy sauce, orange juice, lemon zest, sugar and vinegar and bring to the boil. Cook for 2–3 minutes, then add the five spice powder and oyster mushrooms and mix together over a moderate heat for 1 minute.

Toss with hot pasta, season and sprinkle with toasted sesame seeds. Serve the crispy leeks on the side.

• This sauce can also be served with cold pasta.

Mushroom sauce with dried porcini

Dried porcini have a wonderful woody flavour and are justifiably considered a great delicacy. Serve this sauce with tagliatelle, a crisp green salad and focaccia bread.

25 g (1 oz) dried porcini
150 ml (5 fl oz) dry white wine
100 g (4 oz) butter
1 onion, chopped
1 clove garlic, peeled and crushed
1 tablespoon fresh parsley, chopped
1 tablespoon fresh basil leaves,
torn into ribbons
1 teaspoon tomato purée

450 g (1 lb) mixed fresh mushrooms
(button, oyster and flat), roughly chopped,
except the oyster mushrooms
Salt and freshly ground black pepper
1 tablespoon plain flour
125 ml (4 fl oz) fresh meat stock
(available in supermarkets)
1 teaspoon Dijon mustard
Freshly grated Parmesan

Put the dried porcini in a bowl, cover with hot water and soak for 30 minutes. Drain, taking care to leave any grit behind at the bottom of the bowl, and reserve 120 ml (4 fl oz) of the liquid.

In a small saucepan heat the wine and simmer for 4 minutes, then set aside.

Melt half the butter in a heavy-based pan and gently cook the onion until soft but not browned. Add the garlic and herbs and cook for 1 minute, then add the tomato purée and cook for a further 30 seconds. Stir in the drained porcini and sauté for 5 minutes, then add the fresh mushrooms and cook over a moderate heat for 5 minutes, turning the mushrooms regularly. Season, lower the heat and cook for another 5 minutes.

Meanwhile, melt the remaining butter in a heavy saucepan and mix in the flour. Remove the pan from the heat and carefully stir in the stock and the reserved porcini soaking liquid. Add the wine. Cook, stirring, for 10 minutes. Stir in the mustard. Pour over the mushrooms and blend together well. Toss with hot pasta, season and sprinkle with Parmesan.

Summer sauce

This low-calorie sauce is full of natural goodness. Try it with farfalle or spaghetti, and a crisp green salad.

• Make well in advance of serving so the flavours have time to blend.

1 kg (2 1/4 lb) ripe plum tomatoes,
skinned (see page 17), seeded and chopped
6 tablespoons extra virgin olive oil
1/2 tablespoon fresh oregano, chopped
2 tablespoons fresh basil, chopped

2 tablespoons fresh parsley, chopped
2 tablespoons pitted black olives, chopped
2 cloves garlic, peeled and finely chopped
Salt and freshly ground black pepper
1/2 teaspoon sugar

Put all the ingredients in a large bowl and mix together well. Allow the sauce to stand at room temperature for at least 2 hours, then season and toss with hot pasta.

SPICY HERB SAUCE

This delicious sauce has a spicy, Middle Eastern flavour. Serve with penne or macaroni, and a lettuce and cucumber salad.

4 tablespoons olive oil	1/2 teaspoon ground cinnamon
2 cloves garlic, peeled and chopped	1 tablespoon lemon juice
1 onion, finely chopped	Salt and freshly ground black pepper
2 tablespoons fresh parsley, chopped	1 tablespoon fresh coriander, chopped
2 tablespoons fresh mint, chopped	1-2 tablespoons pine nuts, toasted (see page 17)

Heat the oil in a heavy-based pan and fry the garlic and onion for 5 minutes or until golden. Add the parsley, mint, cinnamon and lemon juice and mix together well. Season, toss with hot pasta and sprinkle with coriander and pine nuts.

• This sauce can also be served with cold pasta.

RED ONION AND BLACK OLIVE SAUCE

This colourful sauce has a delicate flavour tinged with a mild sweetness. Try it with fettuccine, linguine or spaghetti, and a watercress salad.

4 tablespoons olive oil	2 tablespoons pitted black olives, halved
2 red onions, halved and sliced	Salt and freshly ground pepper
1 teaspoon sugar	15 g (1/2 oz) butter
3 tablespoons balsamic vinegar	1 tablespoon fresh parsley, chopped

Heat the oil in a heavy-based pan and stir in the onions to coat them with oil, then sprinkle with the sugar and cook for 5 minutes or until translucent. Add the vinegar and olives, season and simmer for a further 2 minutes.

Remove from the heat and stir in the butter. Sprinkle with parsley, then check the seasoning and toss with hot pasta.

• This sauce can also be served with cold pasta.

PEA, PANCETTA AND CREAM SAUCE

This is a light, refreshing sauce where each flavour comes through individually. Try it with fusilli or spaghetti.

1 tablespoon olive oil	350 ml (12 fl oz) double cream
1 thick slice pancetta, diced	15 g (1/2 oz) fresh basil leaves, torn into strips
1 onion, finely chopped	Salt and freshly ground black pepper
1 clove garlic, peeled and chopped	Freshly grated Parmesan
350 g (12 oz) frozen peas	

Heat the oil in a heavy-based pan and fry the pancetta for 1 minute. Add the onion and garlic and fry for 3–4 minutes or until soft.

Meanwhile, cook the peas in a pan of boiling salted water, drain and add to the pancetta mixture. Then pour in the cream and simmer for 5 minutes.

Stir in the basil and season. Toss with hot pasta and sprinkle with Parmesan.

TOMATO, ROCKET AND BASIL SAUCE

This is a classic combination of fresh summer ingredients. Serve with a tubular pasta such as rigatoni or penne.

• This sauce needs to stand for at least 2–3 hours to enhance the flavours.

6 tablespoons extra virgin olive oil	4 cloves garlic, finely chopped
450 g (1 lb) ripe tomatoes, skinned	1/2 teaspoon caster sugar
(see page 17), seeded and roughly chopped	1/2 teaspoon red wine vinegar
40 g (1 1/2 oz) rocket, roughly chopped	Salt and freshly ground black pepper
1 tablespoon fresh basil, roughly chopped	

Combine all the ingredients in a large bowl and leave to stand at room temperature for 2–3 hours.

Toss with hot pasta and serve.

• This sauce can also be served with cold pasta.

BROCCOLI AND TOASTED BREADCRUMB SAUCE

A tasty combination of ingredients with a lovely crunchy topping. Excellent with conchiglie or fusilli.

450 g (1 lb) small broccoli florets	1 tablespoon lemon juice
4 tablespoons extra virgin olive oil	Salt and freshly ground pepper
3 cloves garlic, peeled and crushed	2 tablespoons pine nuts, toasted (see page 17)
100 g (4 oz) dried breadcrumbs	
50 g (2 oz) Parmesan, freshly grated,	
plus more for serving	

Steam the broccoli for 3–4 minutes or until tender, then set aside in a warm bowl.

Heat the oil in a heavy-based pan and fry the garlic for 30 seconds. Add the breadcrumbs and Parmesan and, stirring constantly, fry for 2–3 minutes or until crunchy and golden.

Sprinkle the broccoli with lemon juice, then top with the breadcrumb mixture. Season and sprinkle with more Parmesan and the pine nuts. Toss with hot pasta and serve.

Right: Roasted Vegetable Sauce

LEEK, PROSCIUTTO AND CREAM SAUCE

The distinctive taste of prosciutto goes well with the more delicate flavours of leeks and cream. Try this sauce with spaghetti or linguine.

250 g (9 oz) unsalted butter
5 medium-sized leeks, cut into 5 mm
(1/4 inch) slices
4 shallots, sliced
4 cloves garlic, peeled and crushed
300 ml (10 fl oz) double cream

175 ml (6 fl oz) fresh chicken stock
(available from supermarkets)
40 g (1 1/2 oz) prosciutto, cut into strips
Salt and freshly ground black pepper
2 tablespoons fresh parsley, chopped

Melt the butter in a heavy-based pan. Add the leeks, shallots and garlic and cook for 5 minutes or until soft.

Stir in the cream, stock and prosciutto and bring to the boil, then lower the heat and simmer gently for 20 minutes. Season, add the parsley and toss with hot pasta.

BROAD BEAN AND HAM SAUCE

This is a colourful, full-bodied sauce with a wonderful texture. Serve with penne or spaghetti.

2 tablespoons olive oil
4 rashers smoked bacon, rind removed, diced
1 onion, chopped
2 cloves garlic, peeled and crushed
2 sticks celery, chopped

450 g (1 lb) tender, young and fresh broad beans or frozen broad beans
100 g (4 oz) cooked ham, cut into strips
3 tablespoons fresh parsley, chopped
Salt and freshly ground black pepper

Heat the oil in a heavy-based pan and cook the bacon, onion, garlic and celery gently for 10–12 minutes.

Meanwhile, cook the broad beans in a pan of boiling salted water for 5 minutes or until tender. Drain and add to the vegetables. Stir in the ham, then sprinkle with parsley, season and toss with hot pasta.

PASTA SALAD WITH SPRING VEGETABLES

The sauce for this attractive salad is deliciously tangy. Just the thing for a hot summer's day.

100 g (4 oz) fusilli
1 tablespoon olive oil
75 g (3 oz) asparagus tips
50 g (2 oz) peas (shelled fresh or frozen)
1 spear of broccoli, cut into small florets

300 ml (10 fl oz) crème fraîche
2 tablespoons creamed horseradish sauce
1 tablespoon lemon juice
Salt and freshly ground black pepper
2 heaped tablespoons fresh chives, chopped

Cook the pasta, drain and put into a large bowl. Toss with the olive oil and put to one side.

Steam the vegetables for 4 minutes, then refresh with cold water to keep the colour.

Combine the crème fraîche, horseradish sauce and lemon juice in a bowl. Add to the pasta, season and mix well. Gently toss in the vegetables and sprinkle with chopped chives.

- Try young, fresh broad beans in place of peas.
- For extra colour throw in a handful of pitted black olives.
- A little fresh mint, coarsely chopped, is delicious mixed into the salad.
- This sauce is best served at room temperature – do not keep it in the refrigerator.

FENNEL AND PANCETTA SAUCE

The distinctive flavours of pancetta and fennel complement each other to perfection. Serve with brandelle or maltagliati.

1 tablespoon olive oil
2 fennel bulbs, outer leaves removed, sliced
1 onion, sliced
2 1/2 tablespoons pancetta, chopped
1 kg (2 1/4 lb) ripe tomatoes, skinned (see page 17), seeded and chopped

15 g (1/2 oz) fresh basil leaves, torn into strips
1 tablespoon lemon juice
Salt and freshly ground black pepper
A few strips of basil to garnish

Heat the olive oil in a heavy-based pan and sauté the fennel, onion and pancetta for 6 minutes. Add the tomatoes and basil and cook for 3–4 minutes or until soft. Stir in the lemon juice, season, sprinkle with basil and toss with hot pasta.

Right: Red Onion and Black Olive Sauce

Above: Courgette, Garlic and Toasted Breadcrumb Sauce

AUBERGINE SAUCE

This refreshing, full-bodied sauce has a delicate flavour. Serve with pappardelle or large tagliatelle.

• The aubergine needs an hour's preparation before you start cooking the sauce.

1 large aubergine, peeled and sliced	*1 tablespoon lemon juice*
Salt	*2 tablespoons pine nuts, toasted*
4 tablespoons olive oil	*(see page 17)*
2 cloves garlic, peeled and crushed	*2 tablespoons sunflower seeds, toasted*
2 tablespoons sun-dried tomato paste	*(see page 17)*
5 tomatoes, skinned (see page 17),	*1 teaspoon dried chilli flakes*
seeded and chopped	*Salt and freshly ground black pepper*
3 sun-dried tomatoes, reconstituted in warm	*4 tablespoons fresh coriander, chopped*
water or drained of oil, then cut into strips	

Sprinkle the aubergine slices with salt and leave to sweat for 1 hour. Then dry and dice.

Heat the olive oil in a heavy-based pan and fry the garlic for 30 seconds. Stir in the sun-dried tomato paste and then the aubergine dice and cook gently for 1 minute or until tender but not mushy. Add the tomatoes, sun-dried tomatoes, lemon juice, pine nuts, seeds and chilli flakes and mix together well. Season, and cook for 5 minutes.

Sprinkle with coriander, then toss with hot pasta.

• This sauce can also be served with cold pasta.

SPINACH SAUCE

Try this light creamy sauce with festoni or pappardelle.

25 g (1 oz) spinach leaves, washed and	*250 ml (8 fl oz) milk*
tough stalks removed	*Good pinch of nutmeg, freshly grated*
25 g (1 oz) butter	*2 tablespoons Parmesan, freshly grated*
1 clove garlic, peeled and crushed	*Salt and freshly ground black pepper*
40 g (1 1/2 oz) plain flour	

Cook the wet spinach for 4–5 minutes, then press out excess water, reserving 2 tablespoons of the liquid.

Melt the butter in a small saucepan, add the garlic and cook for 30 seconds. Add the flour and stir to a paste. Still stirring, pour in the milk a little at a time. Bring to the boil and simmer for 2–3 minutes, stirring occasionally. Add the nutmeg, spinach, reserved spinach liquid and Parmesan, then transfer the mixture to a food processor and blend for 30 seconds. Season and toss with hot pasta.

COURGETTE, GARLIC AND TOASTED BREADCRUMB SAUCE

This sauce not only tastes good but smells wonderful too. Try it with farfalle or fusilli.

5 tablespoons olive oil	*5 tablespoons natural dried breadcrumbs*
3 cloves garlic, peeled and chopped	*(available from supermarkets)*
450 g (1 lb) courgettes, diced	*2 tablespoons Parmesan, freshly grated*
Salt and freshly ground black pepper	

Heat 3 tablespoons of the oil in a heavy-based pan, add 2 cloves of garlic and the courgettes and season. Toss until the courgettes begin to soften around the edges. Remove and drain on kitchen paper.

Add the remaining oil to the pan and gently fry the breadcrumbs with the remaining garlic for 1 minute or until they turn golden. Return the courgettes to the pan and gently fry for 1 minute, stirring well. Season, toss with hot pasta and sprinkle with Parmesan.

YELLOW PEPPER BUTTER SAUCE

This smooth, sophisticated sauce has a lovely, delicate flavour. Delicious with fettuccine, and a rocket salad.

8 yellow peppers, skinned (see page 17)	*Salt and freshly ground black pepper*
250 g (9 oz) salted butter, cut into chunks	*1 tablespoon fresh basil leaves, torn into strips*

Place the peppers and butter in a food processor and blend until smooth. Transfer the mixture to a small saucepan and heat gently for 3–4 minutes. Season, toss with hot pasta and sprinkle with basil.

Roasted Vegetable Sauce

gutsy vegetable sauce, topped with melted mozzarella. Serve with
enne, gnocchetti rigati or conchiglie, and a crisp green salad.

eheat the oven to 230°C, 450°F, Gas Mark 8.

courgettes, cut into 2.5 cm (1 inch) cubes	15 g (¹/2 oz) fresh basil leaves,
0 g (1 lb) large ripe tomatoes,	roughly chopped
ved or cut into rough slices,	Salt and freshly ground black pepper
pending on the size of the tomato	3 ¹/2 tablespoons extra virgin olive oil
red pepper, cut into rough slices	100 g (4 oz) mozzarella cheese,
ellow pepper, cut into rough slices	roughly grated
small aubergines, cut into rough slices	5 leaves fresh basil, torn into strips
cloves garlic, peeled and chopped	

read the vegetables on a baking tray and sprinkle with the garlic,
opped basil, salt and pepper. Sprinkle the oil over the vegetables and
ix well to ensure they are evenly coated. Roast for ¹/2 hour.

move the tray from the oven and sprinkle the mozzarella and basil
rips over the hot vegetables. Toss with hot pasta, season and serve.

This sauce can also be served with cold pasta.

Puttanesca Sauce

erived from the back streets of Naples, this gutsy sauce can be served
th spaghetti, bucatini or penne rigate.

ablespoons extra virgin olive oil	2 tablespoons tomato purée
loves garlic, peeled and finely chopped	1 tablespoon capers, rinsed and drained
large leaves fresh basil, chopped	450 g (1 lb) ripe tomatoes, skinned
resh red chilli, seeded and finely chopped	(see page 17), seeded and chopped
g (2 oz) canned anchovies, drained	Salt and freshly ground black pepper
5 g (6 oz) pitted black olives,	Freshly grated Parmesan
ghly chopped	

eat the oil in a heavy-based pan and gently fry the garlic, basil and
illi for 1 minute – take care not to burn the garlic. Add the remaining
gredients, season and simmer for 45 minutes, stirring occasionally.

oss with hot pasta and sprinkle with Parmesan.

Flageolet Bean and Ham Sauce

A strong-flavoured, rustic sauce. Try it with bucatini or spaghetti.

• Soak beans in water overnight.

150 g (5 oz) dried flageolet beans,	1 tablespoon fresh sage, chopped
soaked overnight	1 tablespoon fresh rosemary, chopped
4 tablespoons olive oil	1 teaspoon dried chilli flakes
100 g (4 oz) cooked ham, cut into fine strips	2 tablespoons dry white wine
2 cloves garlic, peeled and chopped	75 g (3 oz) pecorino cheese, freshly grated
1 tablespoon fresh parsley, chopped	Salt and freshly ground black pepper

Drain the beans, then cook in boiling salted water for 1 hour or until
tender. Drain and set aside.

Heat the oil in a heavy-based frying pan and fry the ham, garlic, herbs
and chilli flakes for 5 minutes. Add the beans and wine and cook for a
further 6–7 minutes, stirring occasionally. If the mixture becomes too
dry, add a little more wine or water.

Stir in the cheese, season and toss with hot pasta.

Wilted Rocket and Parmesan Sauce

The unique flavour of rocket is accentuated when it is cooked. Serve with linguine or spaghetti.

2 tablespoons virgin olive oil
1 clove garlic, peeled and crushed
100 g (4 oz) rocket leaves

Salt and freshly ground black pepper
25 g (1 oz) Parmesan,
freshly cut into shavings

Gently heat the oil in a heavy-based pan over a moderate heat, add the garlic and fry for 30 seconds or until pale golden. Remove the garlic with a slotted spoon and discard. Add the rocket and toss around to ensure all the leaves are coated with garlic-flavoured oil, then cook for 1 minute or until soft.

Toss with hot pasta, season and stir in the Parmesan.

Fresh Beetroot Sauce

This colourful sauce looks amazing with a beetroot-based pasta.

5 medium-sized beetroot, cooked,
peeled and cut into cubes
6 tablespoons virgin olive oil
2 heaped tablespoons fresh basil leaves,
torn into pieces

Juice of 1/2 lemon
TO FINISH
Salt and freshly ground black pepper
50 g (2 oz) Parmesan, freshly cut into shavings

Toss all the ingredients with hot or cold pasta, season and sprinkle with Parmesan shavings.

Tomato Sauce

An all time classic! There's no substitute for a really tasty tomato sauce. Serve with any kind of pasta, and a crisp green salad.

1 tablespoon olive oil
1–2 cloves garlic, peeled and crushed
450 g (1 lb) ripe tomatoes, skinned
(see page 17) and chopped, or 800 g
(1 3/4 lb) canned tomatoes,
drained and chopped
1 teaspoon sugar

1 tablespoon fresh parsley, chopped
1 tablespoon fresh basil, chopped
Salt and freshly ground black pepper
1 teaspoon tomato purée
2 tablespoons red wine
Freshly grated Parmesan

Heat the oil in a saucepan and fry the garlic for 30 seconds. Add the tomatoes, sugar and herbs, then season. Simmer for 10 minutes. Add the tomato purée and wine and simmer for a further 15 minutes or until the sauce thickens and sweetens – taste to check.

Season, toss with hot pasta and sprinkle with Parmesan.

• This recipe makes aproximately 900 ml (1 1/2 pints) of sauce.

• This sauce can also be served with cold pasta.

FISH SAUCES

All recipes are for four people.

TUNA, LEMON AND CAPER SAUCE

last-minute supper dish. Serve with farfalle, plus a salad of tomatoes
d black olives.

5 ml (4 fl oz) double cream	parsley, chopped
ablespoons lemon juice	2 teaspoons capers, drained and rinsed
love garlic, peeled and crushed	1/4 teaspoon cayenne pepper
0 g (7 oz) canned tuna, drained	Freshly ground black pepper
/2 tablespoons fresh flat leaf	1 lemon, cut into wedges

t the cream, lemon juice and garlic in a food processor and blend for
) seconds. Transfer the mixture to a bowl, add the tuna, 2 tablespoons
the parsley and the capers, and mix together well. Sprinkle with the
yenne and black pepper.

ss with hot pasta, then sprinkle with the remaining parsley and
corate with wedges of lemon.

CAVIAR AND CREME FRAICHE SAUCE

r the unashamedly indulgent! This sophisticated combination can be
rved with a delicate pasta, such as fresh linguine or fettuccine.

ablespoons crème fraîche	Freshly ground black pepper
g (1/2 oz) fresh chives, chopped	100 g (4 oz) salmon roe caviar

t the crème fraîche and chives in a heavy-based saucepan and gently
arm over a low heat. Remove from the heat and season with pepper.

ss with hot pasta and top each serving with a spoonful of caviar.

This sauce can also be served with cold fusilli or farfalle.

PRAWN, GARLIC AND CREAM SAUCE

ull of flavour, this delicious sauce is perfect for a dinner party.
rve with farfalle or fusilli, and a spinach and tomato salad.

ablespoons double cream	1 tablespooon fresh parsley, chopped
5 g (6 oz) cream cheese with	1 teaspoon lemon zest, grated
rlic and herbs	Freshly ground black pepper
5 g (6 oz) cooked peeled prawns	

eat the cream and cheese in a heavy-based saucepan over a low heat,
rring constantly. As soon as the mixture is smooth, turn up the
at and bring to the boil. Remove from the heat and stir in the rest
the ingredients.

ss with hot pasta and serve.

SMOKED SALMON AND WHISKY SAUCE

Just the thing for an impromptu supper party. Serve with farfalle, and a
rocket salad.

75 g (3 oz) butter	1–2 teaspoons whisky
250 g (9 oz) smoked salmon,	(no more – it can be overpowering)
cut into small strips	6 tablespoons crème fraîche
	Freshly ground black pepper

Melt the butter in a heavy-based pan over a moderate heat and toss
the salmon for a few seconds. Almost immediately stir in the whisky
followed by the crème fraîche.

Season with pepper and toss with hot pasta.

SPICY FISH SAUCE

This gutsy sauce not only looks magnificent but tastes wonderful too.
Serve with bucatini, and a crisp green salad.

800 g (1 3/4 lb) canned	1 fish stock cube, dissolved in 100 ml
ready-chopped tomatoes	(3 1/2 fl oz) hot water
5 tablespoons fresh parsley, plus more to	2 tablespoons Pernod
garnish, roughly chopped	Salt and freshly ground black pepper
1 tablespoon fresh dill, roughly chopped	450 g (1 lb) mixed seafood: squid
1 small fresh chilli, seeded and finely	cut into 1 cm (1/2 inch) rings,
chopped	monkfish cut into 2.5 cm (1 inch) cubes,
3 cloves garlic, peeled and roughly	and large prawns in their shells
chopped	(shells add flavour) or peeled

Put all the ingredients except the seafood in a food processor and blend
for 1 minute. Pour into a saucepan, bring to the boil and simmer for 10
minutes. Add the seafood and simmer for a further 4 minutes. Toss with
hot pasta and sprinkle with parsley.

• If any of the recommended seafood is unavailable, substitute with a
firm-fleshed white fish.

• For the ultimate indulgence, add chunks of fresh lobster.

CRAB AND GINGER SAUCE

The delicate flavour of crab is sharpened by the addition of ginger. Delicious with fusilli or fafalle, and a Chinese leaf salad.

150 g (5 oz) butter
Small bunch spring onions, trimmed and chopped
7.5–10 cm (3–4 inch) piece fresh root ginger, peeled and grated
250 ml (8 fl oz) double cream

1 tablespoon sherry
4 tablespoons dry white wine
Salt and freshly ground black pepper
175 g (6 oz) white crabmeat, flaked
1 tablespoon chopped fresh coriander

Melt the butter in a heavy-based saucepan and fry the spring onions and ginger until golden. Pour on the cream, sherry and wine, season and stir well. Bring to the boil and cook for 5 minutes or until the sauce thickens, then stir in the crabmeat.

Toss with hot pasta and sprinkle with coriander.

VONGOLE SAUCE

One of the best – a classic from Naples. Excellent with spaghetti or tagliolini, and a fennel salad dressed with extra virgin olive oil and fresh lemon juice.

3 tablespoons olive oil
3 cloves garlic, peeled and chopped
4 large ripe tomatoes, skinned (see page 17), seeded and chopped

450 g (1 lb) canned vongole, drained, or 1.35 kg (3 lb) fresh vongole (venus clams) in their shells, well scrubbed
Salt and freshly ground black pepper
3 tablespoons fresh parsley, chopped

Heat the oil in a heavy-based pan and sauté the garlic for 30 seconds. Add the tomatoes and cook for 5 minutes, stirring occasionally. Stir in canned vongole and cook for a further 2 minutes. If using fresh vongole, cook for 5 minutes or until the shells are all open (discard any that remain closed).

Season, toss with hot pasta and sprinkle with parsley.

• This sauce can also be served with cold pasta.

ANCHOVY, RED PEPPER AND CHILLI SAUCE

A colourful sauce with a wonderful, strong flavour. Try it with conchiglie, or serve as a starter.

Preheat the oven to 200°C, 400°F, Gas Mark 6.

5 red peppers
125 ml (4 fl oz) olive oil
3 cloves garlic, peeled and crushed
1 fresh red chilli, finely chopped
2 x 50 g (2 oz) cans anchovy fillets, drained

5 tablespoons fresh parsley, chopped
Freshly ground black pepper
Freshly grated Parmesan

Put the peppers on a baking sheet and roast for 25–30 minutes or until their skins turn black. Put them in a plastic bag, seal and allow to cool. Then, over a bowl, peel, seed, and cut into 1 cm (1/2 inch) strips. Reserve the juices.

Heat the oil in a heavy-based pan and over a moderate heat sauté the garlic and chilli for 1 minute. Add the peppers with any reserved juice and the anchovies and sauté for a further 2–3 minutes. Stir in the parsley and season with pepper. Toss with hot pasta and sprinkle with Parmesan.

• This sauce can also be served with cold pasta, but leave out the Parmesan.

SCALLOPS WITH BLACK PASTA

Serve the scallops with black ink pasta and a fresh green salad to create an eye-catching effect.

2 tablespoons light olive oil
12 large scallops, corals removed, sliced in half horizontally
300 ml (10 fl oz) dry white vermouth

1–2 teaspoons balsamic vinegar
Salt and freshly ground black pepper
15 g (1/2 oz) butter
2 tablespoons fresh flat leaf parsley, chopped

Pour the oil into a very hot pan and quickly fry the scallops on both sides until golden but not quite cooked. Remove and set aside in a warm dish.

Add the wine to the pan and stir and scrape to mix with the residue from the scallops. Bring the liquid to the boil and simmer until reduced by about half the original quantity. Add the vinegar and season, then return the scallops to the pan and cook for 1 minute. Gently stir in the butter. Pour the sauce over hot pasta and sprinkle with parsley.

CALLOPS WITH STIR-FRIED
ATATOUILLE

he flavour of fresh scallops blends beautifully with a ratatouille of
esh vegetables. Serve with tagliatelle.

scallops, corals removed	5 mm x 5 cm (¹/4 x 2 inch) strips
ablespoons olive oil	3 courgettes, thinly sliced and cut into
t and freshly ground black pepper	5 mm x 5 cm (¹/4 x 2 inch) strips
love garlic, peeled and crushed	1 wineglass dry white wine
mall red onion, cut into thin slices	1 tablespoon tomato purée
ed pepper, cut into very thin strips	10 leaves fresh basil, chopped
ubergine, thinly sliced and cut into	Juice of 1 large lemon

ghtly brush the scallops with olive oil, season with a little black
pper and set aside.

eat the remaining oil in a heavy-based, deep-sided pan and gently
uté the garlic, onion and red pepper. When the mixture begins to
ften add the aubergine and courgettes. Season and cook for a further
5 minutes or until the vegetables are tender but not mushy. Pour in
e wine, then add tomato purée and basil and stir well. Keep hot.

eat a heavy-based frying pan until it starts to smoke. Throw in the
allops and brown them lightly on both sides, then lower the heat
d cook for 3–4 minutes, turning once or twice to ensure they
ok evenly.

ss the ratatouille with hot pasta and serve with the scallops on top.
ueeze lemon juice over the dish and serve.

EAFOOD SAUCE

st the sauce for a hot summer day. Serve with farfalle or conchiglie.

5 g (8 oz) pasta, cooked	2 tablespoons fresh parsley, chopped
5 g (8 oz) mixed cooked shellfish:	1 teaspoon dried thyme or oregano
wns, mussels, squid and clams	6 tablespoons olive oil
5 g (8 oz) sugar snap peas,	1 tablespoon lemon juice
ked for 2–3 minutes	Salt and freshly ground black pepper
aby gherkins, chopped	1 tablespoon capers, drained
ablespoons fresh basil, chopped	

ix the pasta with the shellfish, sugar snap peas and gherkins.

a separate bowl combine the herbs, olive oil and lemon juice.
ss with the pasta. Season and sprinkle with capers.

Above: *Scallops with Black Pasta*

Squid and tomato sauce

This richly satisfying sauce has a slightly Oriental flavour. Serve with
spaghetti or any long, round pasta.

5 tablespoons olive oil	450 g (1 lb) squid, cleaned and cut into rings
1 clove garlic, peeled and crushed	(leave the tentacles whole)
1 small fresh red chilli, seeded and	Salt and freshly ground black pepper
finely chopped	2–3 tablespoons fresh coriander, chopped
900 g (2 lb) ripe tomatoes, skinned	
(see page 17), seeded and finely chopped	

Heat the oil in a heavy-based pan and sauté the garlic and chilli for 30
seconds. Add the tomatoes and simmer for 5 minutes, stirring
occasionally. Then add the squid and simmer for a further 2 minutes.

Season, stir in the coriander and toss with hot pasta.

SQUID, WINE AND HERB SAUCE

Wonderfully fishy and garlicky, this is an excellent sauce to serve with vermicelli or tagliolini.

tablespoons olive oil	2 wineglasses red wine
small onion, chopped	600 ml (1 pint) good fish stock
tablespoons fresh flat leaf	Salt and freshly ground black pepper
parsley, chopped	2 tablespoons fresh basil, chopped
cloves garlic, peeled and chopped	2 tablespoons fresh chives, chopped
00 g (1 lb) squid, cleaned and cut	
to rings (leave the tentacles whole)	

Heat the oil in a heavy-based pan over a moderate heat and sauté the onion until soft. Add the parsley and garlic and cook for 1 minute, stirring occasionally. Put in the squid, turn up the heat and and sauté for 2 minutes, then lower the heat, add the wine and fish stock, and simmer very gently for 1–1 1/2 hours or until the squid is tender.

Toss with hot pasta, season and sprinkle with basil and chives.

PRAWN, MANGE TOUT AND FRESH MINT SAUCE

Minty, creamy and crunchy, try this delicious sauce with tortiglioni penette.

tablespoons olive oil	3 tablespoons fresh mint leaves, chopped
cloves garlic, peeled and chopped	175 ml (6 fl oz) crème fraîche
75 g (6 oz) mange tout	Salt and freshly ground black pepper
0 g (12 oz) shelled prawns	

Gently heat the oil in a saucepan, add the garlic and mange tout and cook for 1 minute. Add the remaining ingredients, season and cook for another minute, then toss with hot pasta.

To serve cold, use fromage frais instead of crème fraîche. Stir into the sauce when it is cooked and cool.

LOBSTER AND CHEESE SAUCE

This sauce has a subtle, fishy flavour. Try it with fettuccine or spaghetti.

tablespoon olive oil	and cut into 1 cm (1/2 inch) pieces
tablespoon onion, chopped	1 tablespoon fresh chives, chopped
wineglass dry white wine	1 tablespoon fresh basil leaves,
heaped tablespoons crème fraîche	torn into strips
g (2 oz) soft garlic cheese	1 tablespoon parsley, chopped
0 g (1 lb) cooked lobster, meat removed	Salt and freshly ground black pepper

Heat the oil in a heavy-based pan and sauté the onion until soft but not brown. Pour in the wine and simmer for 4 minutes. Add the crème fraîche and cheese and bring to the boil, stirring. Simmer until the sauce starts to thicken, then add the lobster meat and heat for 1 minute. Stir in the herbs, season and toss with hot pasta.

TUNA, TOMATO AND BLACK OLIVE SAUCE

Bursting with Mediterranean flavours, this sauce is delicious with penne, and a salad of dandelion leaves.

6 tablespoons olive oil	1 teaspoon green peppercorns,
1 red onion, finely chopped	drained and chopped
3 cloves garlic, peeled and chopped	200 g (7 oz) canned tuna, drained
1 sprig fresh thyme	400 g (14 oz) canned cannelini beans,
400 g (14 oz) canned chopped tomatoes	drained and roughly chopped
2 tablespoons sun-dried tomatoes,	Grated zest of 1 lemon
reconstituted in warm water or	Salt and freshly ground black pepper
drained of oil, then thinly sliced	4 tablespoons fresh parsley, chopped
1 heaped tablespoon pitted	
black olives, chopped	

Heat the oil in a heavy-based, deep-sided pan and sauté the onion with the garlic and thyme until soft. Then turn up the heat, add the canned tomatoes with their juice and cook until the sauce thickens, stirring occasionally. Turn down the heat, stir in the sun-dried tomatoes, olives, peppercorns, tuna, beans and lemon zest and cook for a further 2 minutes.

Toss with hot pasta, season and sprinkle with parsley.

• This sauce can also be served with cold pasta.

TUNA, NUT, CAPER AND LEMON SAUCE

This excellent sauce has a slightly sharp edge and a lovely nutty texture. Serve with farfalle and a green leaf salad.

• This sauce needs to marinate overnight.

Preheat the oven to 180°C, 350°F, Gas Mark 4.

900 g (2 lb) fresh tuna	1/2 teaspoon dried chilli flakes
5 tablespoons olive oil	Grated zest and juice of 2 lemons
50 g (2 oz) pine nuts, toasted (see page 17)	2 tablespoons fresh basil leaves, chopped
2 cloves garlic, peeled and crushed	Salt and freshly ground black pepper
2 tablespoons capers, drained and	
roughly chopped	

Lightly brush the fish with 1 tablespoon of the olive oil and wrap in foil, sealing tightly. Bake for 10–15 minutes, then remove, cool and flake.

Combine the flaked fish with the remaining ingredients in a bowl and mix well. Marinate at room temperature overnight.

Toss with hot pasta and season.

• This sauce can also be served with cold pasta.

SALMON, OLIVE AND BEAN SAUCE

A surprisingly gutsy, full-flavoured sauce that goes well with festone and maltagliati.

Preheat the oven to 190°C, 375°F, Gas Mark 5.

225 g (8 oz) salmon fillet
400 g (14 oz) canned flageolet beans
50 g (2 oz) pitted black olives,
chopped into small pieces

5 tablespoons extra virgin olive oil
Salt and freshly ground black pepper

Lightly oil an ovenproof dish, put in the salmon and bake for 10 minutes. Remove, cool and flake.

Heat the beans in their liquid. Drain and put into a large bowl with the salmon and remaining ingredients. Toss with hot pasta, season and add a dash of extra virgin olive oil.

OYSTER AND CHAMPAGNE SAUCE

The extravagant combination of oysters and champagne is unbeatable! Serve with angel hair or linguini.

25 g (1 oz) butter
2 leeks, finely sliced
250 ml (8 fl oz) champagne
2 dozen oysters, shelled

250 ml (8 fl oz) crème fraîche
Salt and freshly ground black pepper
1 tablespoon fresh chives, chopped

Melt the butter in a large, heavy-based pan. Add the leeks and sauté for 2–3 minutes. Pour in the champagne and heat until the liquid starts to simmer. Add the oysters and cook for 2 minutes, then remove them with a slotted spoon and set aside. Simmer the champagne mixture for 6–7 minutes, then stir in the crème fraîche, season and cook for a further 10 minutes.

Lower the heat, replace the oysters in the sauce and heat for 30 seconds only. Toss with hot pasta and sprinkle with chives.

• Serve in bowls as the sauce may be a little runny.

• Use Sauternes instead of champagne.

Left: Anchovy, Red Pepper and Chilli Sauce

MUSSEL AND SAFFRON CREAM SAUCE

his is a sophisticated sauce where each flavour comes through
dividually. Delicious with spaghettini or tagliolini.

hreads saffron	900 g (2 lb) fresh mussels, scrubbed
0 ml (12 fl oz) crème fraîche	and beards removed
g (2 oz) butter	Salt and freshly ground black pepper
hallots, finely chopped	2 tablespoons fresh chives, chopped
0 ml (8 fl oz) fresh fish stock	
vailable in supermarkets)	

ix the saffron with the crème fraîche and leave to one side.

elt the butter in a large, heavy-based saucepan and sauté the shallots
r 2 minutes. Pour in the stock and bring to simmering point. Add the
ussels, cover the pan and cook for about 6 minutes or until all the
ells are open (discard any mussels that remain closed). Strain the
quid through a large sieve or colander set in a bowl and discard any
npty shells. Put the mussels in another bowl and set aside.

eturn the liquid to the pan and boil until reduced by half the original
uantity. Stir in the crème fraîche and saffron mixture and boil for
further 10 minutes. Lower the heat, season and return the mussels
 the sauce to heat for 30 seconds. Toss with hot pasta and sprinkle
ith chives.

MOKED TROUT, MAYONNAISE AND
ILL SAUCE

his light, summer sauce is excellent with conchiglie, and a crisp
een salad.

0 g (7 oz) fresh mayonnaise	15 g (1/2 oz) fresh chives, chopped
ml (3 fl oz) vinaigrette dressing	15 g (1/2 oz) fresh basil leaves, chopped
tablespoon lemon juice	8 fillets smoked trout
lt and freshly ground black pepper	(available from supermarkets)
g (1/2 oz) fresh dill, chopped	

ss cold cooked pasta with the mayonnaise, then toss again with the
naigrette and once more with the lemon juice and seasoning. Stir in
e chopped herbs, then very carefully fold in the trout, keeping the
eces as large as possible.

ANCHOVY, CREAM AND LEMON SAUCE

This is a delicate sauce with a slightly piquant flavour. Excellent with
tagliolini and a salad of tomato, spinach and hard-boiled egg.

15 g (1/2 oz) butter	Grated zest and juice of 1 lemon
50 g (2 oz) canned anchovy fillets,	250 ml (8 fl oz) crème fraîche
drained and rinsed	Salt and freshly ground black pepper
1 onion, finely chopped	2 tablespoons fresh flat leaf parsley, chopped
1 teaspoon capers, finely chopped	1/4 teaspoon cayenne pepper

Melt the butter in a heavy-based pan and over a very low heat cook
the anchovies for 4 minutes or until they break up, stirring
occasionally. Be careful as they burn very easily. Add the onion and
cook for 5 minutes, then add the capers and lemon zest and juice and
cook for another 5 minutes. Stir in the crème fraîche and cook until
the sauce starts to thicken. Remove from the heat and toss with hot
pasta. Season, sprinkle with parsley and dust with a little cayenne
pepper.

SALMON, NUTMEG AND FENNEL SAUCE

The exquisite taste of salmon is accentuated by the subtle combination
of fennel and nutmeg. Try it with spaghettini.

Preheat the oven to 190°C, 375°F, Gas Mark 5.

350 g (12 oz) salmon fillet	2–3 tablespoons freshly grated
300 ml (10 fl oz) double cream	pecorino cheese
50 g (2 oz) butter	1 medium-sized fennel bulb, thinly sliced
1 wineglass dry white wine	Salt and freshly ground black pepper
3–4 pinches of grated nutmeg	2 tablespoons fresh parsley, chopped

Lightly oil an ovenproof dish, put in the salmon and bake for 10–12
minutes. Remove, cool and flake.

Put the cream, butter, wine and nutmeg in a heavy-based saucepan
and bring to the boil. Add the cheese and fennel, then gently stir in
the salmon.

Toss with hot pasta, season and sprinkle with parsley.

eft: Spicy Fish Sauce

MEAT SAUCES

All recipes are for four people.

BRESAOLA AND GREEN PEPPERCORN SAUCE

The unusual combination of spicy green peppercorns and the delicate flavour of bresaola is out of this world. Serve with linguine or fettuccine, and a lamb's lettuce salad.

15 g (¹/₂ oz) butter
1 clove garlic, peeled and crushed
40 g (1 ¹/₂ oz) bottled green peppercorns, rinsed and drained
50 g (2 oz) bresaola, cut into 1 cm (¹/₂ inch) strips
250 ml (8 fl oz) double cream
Salt and freshly ground black pepper

Melt the butter in a saucepan and gently fry the garlic for 30 seconds or until golden – take care not to burn. Add the peppercorns and fry them for 5–6 minutes or until they pop. Then stir in the bresaola, mixing together well. Pour in the cream, turn up the heat and slowly bring to the boil, then lower the heat and simmer for 2–3 minutes.

Season and toss with hot pasta.

HOT BACON SAUCE

This versatile sauce is similar to a hot vinaigrette dressing. Try it with fusilli or penne.

175 ml (6 fl oz) olive oil
3–4 cloves garlic, peeled and crushed
175 g (6 oz) smoked bacon, rind removed, cut into 5 mm (¹/₄ inch) strips
4 tablespoons balsamic vinegar
1 ¹/₂ tablespoons fresh parsley, chopped
Salt and freshly ground black pepper
Freshly grated Parmesan

Heat half the oil in a large, heavy-based frying pan and gently sauté the garlic for 30 seconds – take care it does not burn. Remove with a slotted spoon, and discard.

Add the bacon to the pan and fry for 4 minutes or until crisp, then pour away all the fat. Scrape the bottom of the pan to loosen the deposits, add the vinegar and stir well. Pour in the remaining oil and, when the sauce is hot, add the parsley. Season, toss with hot pasta and sprinkle with Parmesan.

BOLOGNESE SAUCE

A robust, strong-flavoured sauce. Just the thing to warm you up on a cold, wintery night! Serve with tagliolini or spaghetti.

2 rashers smoked bacon, rind removed
100 g (4 oz) chicken livers (optional)
2 tablespoons olive oil
1 clove garlic, peeled and crushed
1 tablespoon onion, chopped
1 tablespoon carrot, chopped
1 tablespoon celery, chopped
450 g (1 lb) lean minced beef or chopped steak
1 wineglass white wine
2 tablespoons tomato purée
300 ml (10 fl oz) fresh chicken stock (available in supermarkets)
1 bay leaf
1 sprig fresh thyme
1 tablespoon fresh parsley, chopped
6 fennel seeds
Salt and freshly ground black pepper
Freshly grated Parmesan

Finely chop the bacon and chicken livers (if using) in a food processor

Heat the oil in a deep, heavy-based pan and, stirring frequently, sauté the garlic, onion, celery and carrot until soft. Add the chicken livers, bacon and beef and cook for a further 2 minutes, then pour in the wine and add the tomato purée. Stir well and and cook for 2 minutes. Add the chicken stock, herbs and fennel seeds and simmer gently for 1 hour.

Season, toss with hot pasta and sprinkle with Parmesan.

• This is the authentic base for lasagne.

• This sauce freezes well, so make double the quantity and keep some in reserve.

SALAMI AND PEPPERONI SAUCE

This gutsy sauce has a lovely tangy edge to it. Delicious with tagliatelle, and a tomato salad mixed with very finely sliced shallots.

1 tablespoon olive oil
275g (10 oz) jar Italian pepperoni, drained and cut into strips
75g (3 oz) salami, cut into 1 cm
(¹/₂ inch) strips
1 tablespoon capers, rinsed and drained
1 tablespoon fresh parsley, chopped
Freshly ground black pepper

Heat the oil in a heavy-based pan. Add the pepperoni and salami and cook gently for 5 minutes, stirring occasionally. Mix in the capers and parsley and season with pepper. Toss with hot pasta and serve.

PORK, SAFFRON AND BASIL SAUCE

The combination of saffron and pork is a great success!
Serve with orecchiette or penne rigate.

6 strands saffron
300 ml (10 fl oz) fresh chicken stock
(available from supermarkets)
125 ml (4 fl oz) olive oil
1 onion, finely chopped
2 cloves garlic, peeled and crushed
6 leaves fresh basil, chopped
3 tablespoons fresh parsley, chopped

1 tablespoon fresh coriander, chopped
225 g (8 oz) boned loin of pork, minced
1 teaspoon dried chilli flakes
1 tablespoon tomato purée
1 teaspoon soy sauce
Salt and freshly ground black pepper
6 leaves fresh basil, torn into strips

Mix the saffron with the stock and set aside.

Heat the oil in a deep, heavy-based pan over a moderate heat and
gently sauté the onion, garlic, chopped basil, parsley and coriander.
When the onion is soft but not brown, stir in the pork and chilli flakes.
As soon as the meat starts to brown, stir in the tomato purée, soy sauce
and saffron mixture. Season and simmer for 3–4 minutes.

Toss with hot pasta and sprinkle with strips of basil.

PANCETTA AND CHILLI SAUCE

An ingenious sauce with an unusual combination of ingredients.
Serve with penne rigate.

4 tablespoons virgin olive oil
1 onion, chopped
1 fresh red chilli, chopped
175 g (6 oz) pancetta, finely sliced
225 g (8 oz) spring greens,
cut into thin strips

1/2 teaspoon ground cumin
3 medium-sized tomatoes, skinned
(see page 17), seeded and chopped into
1 cm (1/2 inch) pieces
1/2 teaspoon freshly ground black pepper

Heat the oil in a heavy-based pan over a moderate heat and gently
sauté the onion, chilli and pancetta for 4–5 minutes. Add the spring
greens and cumin and, stirring constantly, cook for 1 minute. Add the
tomatoes and cook for another minute.

Season with black pepper and toss with hot pasta.

Left: Bresaola and Green Peppercorn Sauce

PROSCIUTTO AND GOAT'S CHEESE SAUCE

A wickedly moreish sauce! Serve with green noodles.

2 tablespoons light olive oil	175 g (6 oz) goat's cheese, any
2 shallots, finely chopped	rind removed, cut into pieces
2 tablespoons fresh chicken stock	50 g (2 oz) prosciutto, finely diced
(available from supermarkets)	Freshly ground black pepper
2 tablespoons dry white wine	Freshly grated pecorino cheese

Heat the oil in a heavy-based pan and gently fry the shallots until soft but not brown. Add the stock and wine and then the cheese and mix together well. As soon as the cheese has melted, stir in the prosciutto and season with pepper. Toss with hot pasta and sprinkle with pecorino.

FOIE GRAS AND WILD MUSHROOM SAUCE

Creamy and rich, this sauce is best served with fine egg noodles or farfalle.

• This recipe is for 2 people.

25 g (1 oz) dried porcini or 75 g	2 heaped tablespoons crème fraîche
(3 oz) fresh fairy ring mushrooms	50 g (2 oz) terrine de foie gras, or 75 g
or porcini (cèpes)	(3 oz) foie gras, chopped
200 ml (7 fl oz) fresh chicken stock	Freshly ground black pepper
(available in supermarkets)	

If using dried mushrooms, put them in a bowl, cover with water and soak for 1/2 hour. Remove the mushrooms and set aside; discard the water.

Put the stock and crème fraîche in a heavy-based pan and heat gently. Simmer for 2 minutes or until the cream starts to thicken, then add the mushrooms.

Serve hot pasta on individual plates, place the foie gras on top and pour the sauce over it. Season and serve immediately.

ITALIAN SAUSAGE SAUCE WITH LENTILS AND SPINACH

A robust, rich sauce with a wonderful aroma. Serve with a tubular pasta such as rigatoni.

100 g (4 oz) Puy lentils	1 clove garlic, peeled and chopped
1 sprig fresh thyme	450 g (1 lb) baby spinach leaves
1 bay leaf	150 ml (5 fl oz) fresh chicken stock
2 cloves garlic, crushed	(available in supermarkets)
1 wineglass red wine	1 tablespoon tomato purée
4 tablespoons olive oil	Salt and freshly ground black pepper
6 small Italian sausages, pricked	

Put the lentils in a saucepan and add the thyme, bay leaf, 2 crushed garlic, red wine and enough unsalted water to cover. Simmer for about 1/2 hour or until the lentils are tender. Then drain, discard the herbs and set aside.

Meanwhile, heat 2 tablespoons of the oil in a heavy-based frying pan and gently fry the sausages until they are browned on all sides and cooked through. Slice and set aside.

In another pan heat the rest of the oil, add the chopped clove of garlic and sauté for 30 seconds. Then add the spinach, cooked lentils (drained of any excess water), sausage, chicken stock and tomato purée and cook 2–3 minutes, stirring well.

Season and toss with hot pasta.

CREAMED PROSCIUTTO SAUCE

Serve this rich and creamy sauce with penne or fusilli, and a chicory and walnut salad.

50 g (2oz) butter	thick piece, chopped into small pieces
1 onion, finely chopped	Salt and freshly ground black pepper
150 ml (5 fl oz) double cream	75 g (3 oz) Parmesan, freshly grated
50 g (2 oz) prosciutto or Parma ham in a	1 heaped tablespoon fresh parsley, chopped

Melt the butter in a large saucepan and gently fry the onion until soft but not brown. Pour in the cream and bring to the boil. Cook for 1 minute. Stirring constantly, add the prosciutto or Parma ham and seasoning, then the cheese.

Toss with hot pasta and sprinkle with parsley.

Right: Foie Gras and Wild Mushroom Sauce

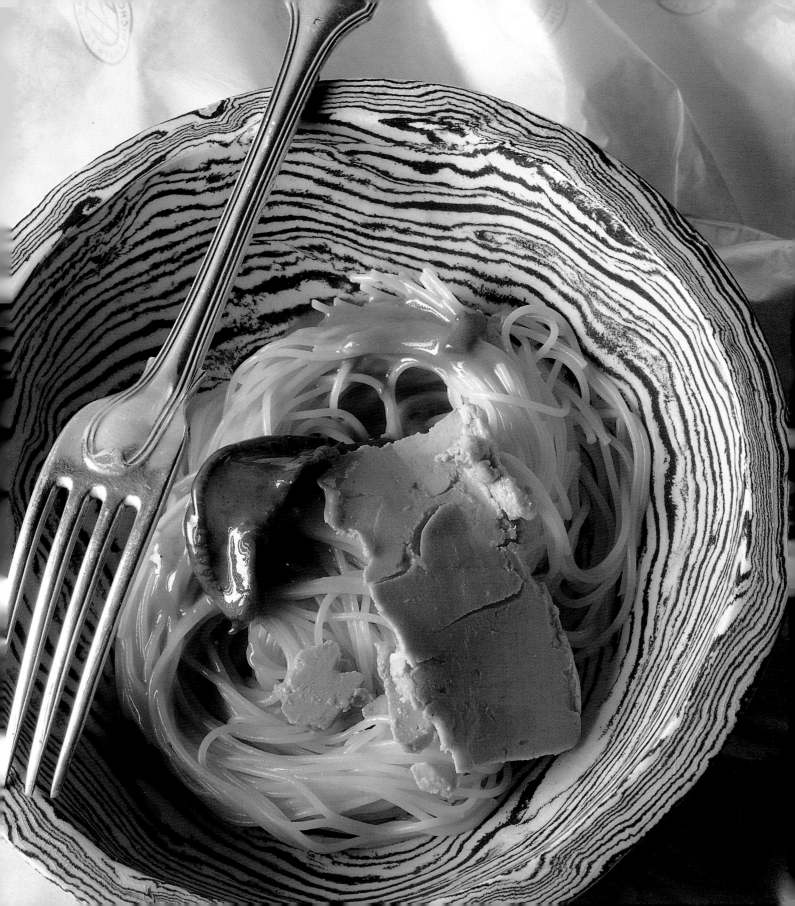

QUAIL, CELERIAC AND MOREL SAUCE

This sophisticated sauce is quick and easy to make. Serve with maltagliati or brandelle.

100 g (4oz) butter	25 g (1oz) dried morels, soaked in water
1 head celeriac, peeled and cut into	for 1/2 hour, then rinsed and sliced
5 mm x 5 cm (1/4 x 2 inch) strips	4 tablespoons fresh chervil, chopped
Breasts of 4 quails (plus livers if obtainable),	Salt and freshly ground black pepper
cut into 5 mm (1/4 inch) strips	Freshly grated pecorino cheese

Heat half of the butter in a heavy-based pan and gently sauté the celeriac for 4–5 minutes or until it softens. Then, using a slotted spoon, transfer the celeriac to a warm plate.

Turn up the heat and sauté the quail breasts for about 3 minutes. Return the celeriac to the pan and add the morels, chervil and remaining butter. Heat for 2 minutes, stirring occasionally. Then season, toss with hot pasta and sprinkle with pecorino cheese.

HARE AND BACON SAUCE

This exceptional sauce is worth every minute of the time it takes to make. Serve with pappardelle.

3 tablespoons olive oil	1 teaspoon fresh thyme, chopped
50 g (2 oz) butter	Salt and freshly ground black pepper
50 g (2 oz) smoked bacon,	1 wineglass dry white wine
rind removed, chopped	1 wineglass red wine
1 small onion, chopped	500 ml (16 fl oz) fresh chicken or veal stock
2 sticks celery, chopped	(available from supermarkets)
900 g (2 lb) meat from a hare,	Freshly grated Parmesan
finely chopped	

Heat the oil and butter in a heavy-based pan over a moderate heat and sauté the bacon, onion and celery until the vegetables are soft. Stir in the meat and thyme and season. As soon as the meat is browned, pour in the wine and simmer until almost completely reduced. Add the stock, then cover and simmer gently for 2–3 hours.

Season, toss with hot pasta and serve with Parmesan.

SPICY SAUSAGE AND TOMATO SAUCE

This full-bodied sauce has a lovely garlicky flavour. Serve with spaghetti or bugatoni, a spinach and mushroom salad and ciabatta bread to mop up the last few drops.

3 tablespoons olive oil	(available in supermarkets)
1 small onion, chopped	600 ml (1 pint) fresh tomato sauce
2 cloves garlic, peeled and crushed	(see page 41) or 400 g (14 oz) canned
3 tablespoons roughly chopped cooked ham	tomatoes, chopped
150 g (5 oz) chorizo sausage, skinned	2 tablespoons fresh parsley, finely chopped
and roughly chopped	Salt and freshly ground black pepper
200 ml (7 fl oz) fresh beef stock	Freshly grated Parmesan

Heat the oil in a heavy-based saucepan, add the onion and garlic and sauté until pale golden. Add the ham and sausage and cook for 3–4 minutes, then add the stock and tomato sauce and simmer for 10–15 minutes, stirring occasionally.

Toss with hot pasta, stir in the parsley, season and sprinkle with Parmesan.

• For a spicier flavour add 1/2 teaspoon dried chilli flakes.

CHICKEN LIVER AND MADEIRA SAUCE

A fabulous combination of ingredients. Serve with conchiglie (large pasta shells), and a salad of lamb's lettuce.

1 tablespoon olive oil	1 clove garlic, peeled and chopped
175 g (6 oz) chicken livers, chopped	1 tablespoon fresh tarragon, chopped
50 g (2 oz) rashers smoked bacon, rind	4 tablespoons madeira
removed, cut across into thin strips (lardons)	Freshly ground black pepper

Put the oil in a heavy-based pan and, over a high heat, quickly fry the livers for 1 minute. Add the bacon and garlic and cook for 3–4 minutes, stirring all the time. Add the tarragon and madeira, stir and cook for another minute.

Toss with hot pasta and season with pepper.

Left: Bolognese Sauce

WILD BOAR SAUCE

If wild boar is unavailable – which it probably is – you can fool your guests by using pork instead. Serve with pappardalle.

• This sauce needs to marinate overnight or for at least 5 hours, and cook for 1–1½ hours.

450 g (1 lb) boned loin of wild boar, cut into cubes, or boned pork loin, cut into 2.5 cm (1 inch) cubes
4 tablespoons olive oil
1 onion, finely chopped
1 carrot, finely chopped
1 stick celery, finely chopped
2 cloves garlic, peeled and crushed
1 tablespoon tomato paste

2 wineglasses red wine
Salt and freshly ground black pepper
Freshly grated pecorino cheese
FOR THE MARINADE
8 juniper berries
1 teaspoon fresh rosemary, chopped
2 wineglasses red wine
1 onion, roughly chopped
4 tablespoons olive oil

Put the minced boar or cubes of pork in a bowl. Mix together the ingredients for the marinade and pour over the meat. Leave to marinate overnight or for a minimum of 5 hours. Drain off the marinating liquid, strain and reserve. (Put the pork in a food processor and chop finely.)

Heat the oil in a heavy-based pan over a moderate heat and sauté the meat, onion, carrot, celery and garlic until the vegetables are soft. Add the wine, marinating liquid and tomato paste and stir well, then simmer for 1–1½ hours or until the meat is very tender. Season, toss with hot pasta and sprinkle with cheese.

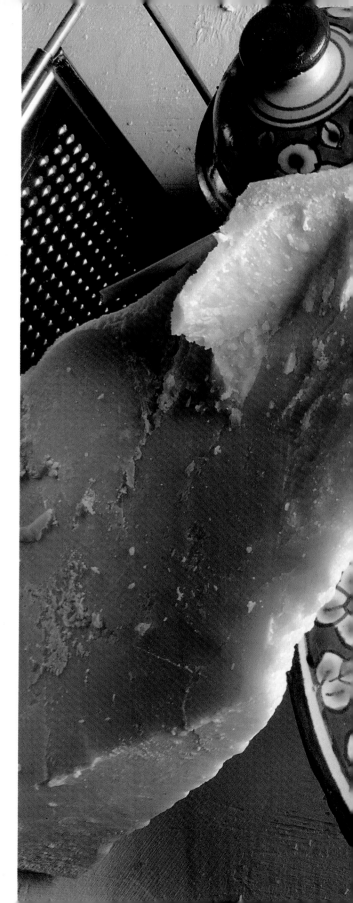

Right: Hot Bacon Sauce

ACKNOWLEDGEMENTS

I would like to thank La Famiglia Restaurant, Loyd Grossman and Orlando Murrin, editor of *Woman & Home*, for donating their delicious recipes.

Also Rose Prince and Jose Luke for testing the recipes and for their own contributions to the book. Their enthusiasm and energy has been inspirational and they have been a joy to work with. Words cannot describe my admiration for Simon Wheeler's splendid photography. As always, he was enormous fun, and kind and considerate towards the rest of the team – a real star.

I would like to thank Elizabeth Gage, Maria Harrington, my son Mark and my assistant Christopher Leach for their enduring support and patience throughout the project.

Last but not least my sincere thanks to the following companies for loaning and supplying food and props for photography:

Italian Delicatessens:
La Picena
5 Walton Street
London SW3 2JD
0171 584 6573

Luigi's Delicatessen
349 Fulham Road
London SW10 9TW
0171 352 7739

Camisa & Son
61 Old Compton Street
London W1V 5PN
0171 437 7610

Suppliers of oils, vinegars and pastes:
Taylor & Lake
44/54 Stewarts Road
London SW8 4DF
0171 622 9156

Suppliers of cheese:
Harvey and Brockless Ltd
44/54 Stewarts Road
London SW8 4DF
0171 720 0976

Shops specialising in kitchen equipment:
Summerill & Bishop
100 Portland Road
London W11 4LN
0171 221 4566

David Mellor
4 Sloane Square
London SW1 8EE
0171 730 4259

Shops and people specialising in decorative tableware, china, glasses and linen:
Verandah
15b Blenheim Crescent
London W11 2EE
0171 792 9289

Ceramica Blue
10 Blenheim Crescent
London W11 1NN
0171 727 0288

William Yeoward
336 King's Road
London SW3 5UR
0171 351 5454

Designers Guild
271 & 277 King's Road
London SW3 5EN
0171 243 7300

Robert Budwig
0181 969 0539
Specialises in table linen

Antique shops specialising in decorative objects:
Lauriance Rogier Antiques
20a Pimlico Road
London SW1 8LJ
0171 823 4780

David Pettifer Antiques
219 King's Road
London SW3 5EJ
0171 352 3088

Ena Green Antiques
566 King's Road
London SW6 2DY
0171 736 2485

Myriad Antiques
131 Portland Road
London W11
0171 229 1709

Guinevere Antiques
578 King's Road
London SW6 2DY
0171 736 2917

Specialist in garden pots and urns
Clifton Little Venice
Garden Antiques and Ornaments
3 Warwick Place
London W9 2PX
0171 289 7894

RECIPE INDEX

This paperback edition first published in 2002 by
Cassell Paperbacks, Cassell & Co
Wellington House, 125 Strand
London, WC2R 0BB

First published in the United Kingdom in 1995 by
George Weidenfeld & Nicolson Limited
The Orion Publishing Group
Orion House
5 Upper St Martin's Lane
London WC2H 9EA

A CIP catalogue record for this book is available
from the British Library

ISBN 1-84188-168-6

Designed by Thumb Design Limited

Printed and bound in Italy